Poetry in Motion

Restore | Reconnect | Renew

Meetali Ohri

ISBN 978-93-5559-015-2
© Meetali Ohri 2022
Published in India 2022 by Pencil

A brand of
One Point Six Technologies Pvt. Ltd.
123, Building J2, Shram Seva Premises,
Wadala Truck Terminal, Wadala (E)
Mumbai 400037, Maharashtra, INDIA
E connect@thepencilapp.com
W www.thepencilapp.com

All rights reserved worldwide

No part of this publication may be reproduced, stored in or introduced into a retrieval system, or transmitted, in any form, or by any means (electronic, mechanical, photocopying, recording or otherwise), without the prior written permission of the Publisher. Any person who commits an unauthorized act in relation to this publication can be liable to criminal prosecution and civil claims for damages.

DISCLAIMER: *The opinions expressed in this book are those of the authors and do not purport to reflect the views of the Publisher.*

Author biography

Meetali Ohri is a Creator and Show Host of "Self Talk Show" Podcast. A Poetry enthusiast, Hobbyist Wildlife Photographer and a keen meditator. Her interest also rests in music. She loves motivating and inspiring people. Her take on life is that If you remove and replace "expectation" with "love" then your life will become as clear as water. To know more about Self Talk Show, visit www.selftalkshow.com

CONTENTS

Acknowledgements

It is with great appreciation that I extend special thanks to my dearest mother who have been a constant support system, her contributions to my work has led to this book. I am so grateful to her. She is my inspiration. I bow to her!

We often forget to thank ourselves because without our strong intention and determination our goals wouldn't fulfil. I thank myself for not giving up, for constantly looking out and in for inspiration, for putting sincere efforts and all the love towards my work and goals.

I would finally like to thank lord divine for blessing me with all the strength and power to share my work with the world and contribute towards its betterment.

A Note to the Reader

Life is not that difficult as it seems to be. We have the power to think, create and serve. Please remember that you are beautiful, strong and amazing. You are a miracle, born to shine, thrive, spread love and contribute to mother earth.

I hope my poetic voice serves the purpose of bringing comfort, inspiration, enthusiasm, realization of being fortunate to be a human and healing to you. I am deeply honoured to serve you.

What You Seek!

Fly high, dive deep

Whatever you do, do it with beam

Dream big and Impossible

Envision it to be possible

'Cause what you seek is seeking you back

Mistakes will happen, do not stop

Obstacles will occur, do not stop

Keep moving, keep moving

'Cause what you seek is seeking you back

In every high, in every low

Never give up, never let go

Listen to your heart, listen to yourself

'Cause what you seek is seeking you back

Be a fighter

Be a challenger

Become a co-creator

Collaborate with lord

shape your life, shape your world

Gather all the strength

Gather all the trust

Believe in yourself

Trust the universe

'Cause what you seek is seeking you back

Oh Lord Divine

Would my saying thank you be enough to let you
know how much grateful I am to you?

You're my life's compass

My detailed direction

My light in the darkness

I love you so much Oh divine

Dear lord, thank you for teaching us the significance
of love and faith

Thank you for holding us during our tough times

Thank you for being so kind

I love you so much Oh divine

Whom am I not to trust you?

Whom am I not to praise you and your creations?

You have created all of us, the universe, the earth

You have loved us in all our lifetimes

You have rescued us during dangerous times

For me there's no heaven no hell only you, only you

Why should I fear when my lord divine is near?

Whom should I fear? Whom should I fear?

I love you so much Oh divine

You talk through us

You walk through us

You breathe through us

You die through us

And move on to the next lifetime through us

Your creations are marvellous

The Universe is spectacular

I love you so much Oh divine

I am short of words

I am short of lines

Because you're so amazing lord divine

You are mysterious yet beautiful

You're in us, you're with us

We are you, you are us!

I love you so much Oh divine, you're the only one on
whom we can rely

My Trusted Ally

My heart is the only place that's always accessible

It is my sacred space, my only temple

My soul's home, holy home

I feel fear no more, no pain no complain

All I feel is love

Love is the only thing I know

It's like wrapping a blanket in chilly winter nights

Love makes me feel uplifted because love is heart
and heart is love

Every heartbeat is like a soothing music

Sometimes rock, most of the times pop

My heart makes me sing and dance

It helps me connect with myself

It always listens, it always responds

It pampers me whenever I want

It takes care of me like my mother do

It nourishes me, makes me strong

It says I have to go on and on and on

As I say I love you to my heart, it responds to me saying I love you more

I am grateful to my lovely heart, keep guiding me every hour

A Moment

A moment of success

A moment of love

A moment of change

A momentary loss

A moment of power to change the world

A moment of realization

A moment of rise and fall

Every fall is a teacher, a pathway to the fulfilment of your dreams

Be mindful, be strong, be brave, be bold

Seize your moment as it holds the ticket to your desired future

Cherish, Celebrate, laud each moment

Every moment is vital

Step forth and open the doors of your heart towards endless possibilities

Accept and flourish in this moment

A beautiful moment, this present moment

Inspiration Is Around You

Inspiration is love

Inspiration is a feeling

Inspiration is like a flowing river

Inspiration is all around you

Inspiration is within you

The road you are walking on, the air you breathe, the sound you hear, the things that surrounds you are astonishingly inspirational

Every moment, every movement, every positive thought is an inspiration

Chirping birds, nature, mother earth, night sky, sunrise, sunset, animal kingdom, oceans, beaches, trees, mountains, forests, homes, music, pen, journal, human mind, even the words are awe-inspiring

Inspiration is connection

Inspiration is experience

Inspiration is awakening

The whole universe is a plethora of inspiration

Inspiration is us, Inspiration is you!

The Present

A gift of today, a key to tomorrow

A platform of karma, A knower of the future

A creator of today, a solution for tomorrow

Transient, Evolving, Transforming, Co-related

A day of sealing your destiny, a day of decision

A time to break free from unnecessary speculations
and living consciously

A time for truth, acceptance, intelligence

A time to act, glorify this present moment and live
joyfully

The Present is a gift of life, a lovely lucid dream

You Matter

You are like a living flower blooming every day

Like a butterfly, you have the power to free yourself
and shine bright as a brand new you

You don't need a rescuer, you are own rescuer

You can sing, dance, fall in love, transform, create,
think, communicate, speak different languages,
protect, discover

Your intentions can bring joy in other's life who are
in sorrow

You can heal anyone who's unwell

You can inspire, seek inspiration, discuss, argue,
detach and attach

Be hopeful, find purpose, find meaning

You can let go, travel through imaginations,
connect, reconnect, create memories, serve others

Can live in harmony with all living creatures, adjust
and readjust, nurture

You can be as stable as mountain, as flowy as river,
as powerful as love

Your determination can turn you into an achiever

You are a divine being of god, you are the universe

So eliminate this thought of unworthiness, go out there, rewrite your story and thrive because "You Matter"

The Healing Power Of Words

As we unveil our pool of hidden pain

To reinvent, to dig deep into that age old liturgy of healing that comes seeing ourselves written into existence

A mirror of our inside story is released onto the sheet

Relieving us from our pain, from the burden allowing us to forgive and be free

As we channel and absorb all the positive and revitalizing energy into us

We open the doors of our heart to heal ourselves with the power of these Impeccable words

Soothing us and asking to rediscover ourselves

These Days

These days, these times

All I think is moving forward

Away from my routine

On a journey to self-exploration

To find meaning, to find positivity

To a place I can relate to

A place where I belong

To watch the night sky undisturbed

Hearing crickets, to meditate in peace

To fall in love with myself all over again

To radiate happiness, feel every sensory fluctuations

To see what others see

To choose to feel emotions

To dive deep into the ocean of calmness and love

To carry my cool everywhere

To chant life changing mantras

To contribute and serve mother earth

To be enlightened!

Sing Your Own Song

Bringing my inner child into picture

As I write my song, I tap into my pool of feelings and emotions that set the tone and environment

Weaving every word like the spider weaves its web

Looking into my personal mythos

My very own designed dictionary

Using memory and sentiments as an icing on the cake

Feeling every word as if it is my own

Pairing the song with similar beats

Singing it loud and jumping around

This is my song, a gift to me

Celebrate yourself, Celebrate your life

Sing your own song and brighten up your inner world!

Be A Believer

Belief is my only constant

Believing is the only key

Believing is love

Believing is free

Believing is power that propels us towards our dreams

What do we have to lose for once in a lifetime to test out the force of belief

Beliefs are our foundation that connect us to the source, to our higher self

Be a believer! Ignite your internal fire! Be the face of the future!

Sweet Laugh

Sitting on my favourite wooden chair, gazing at the morning sky remembering my dad, his talks, his memories brought me a sweet laugh

Always walking with an aura of joy and happiness

A very strong rival in the dessert eating competition

The "2 sips of tea" was a typical "He"

A Mister Chatter, narrator and enthusiast

His laughs were like a lion's roar

His talks were as interesting as he was

Stubborn yet funny, big fan of 80's

He was love, a pure soul

Even though he now is in spirit realm, his memories still manage to bring that lost sweet laugh

Hope

Hope is a good thing

It feeds us with strength, empowers us to walk past our pain and suffering

A four letter word that convince us to believe

Hope strengthen our faith, the only positive emotion that's always in our favour

Hope stamp out fear, love is now always near

Don't bend, Don't break

You are strong, you are brave

"I can do it" is now my slogan

Always be hopeful! Always be hopeful!

Faith

Imagine a world free from war, filled with love, filled with charm

Kind people helping each other

There's no hatred, no jealousy

Only love, only compassion

If this is what our faith say, then be it

A Simple question I always ask

How's your faith? How's your faith?

Inscribed in the bible, a quote says "Faith can move the mountain from here to there"

Have faith, have faith because faith is your propeller, a motivator

Faith is your real home, a true friend

Faith lends you the power to achieve and receive

Which is why I always say, have faith and believe

Self-Love

An act of true love

An act of glory

Shed all the love on you and your story

You don't need people to praise you 'cause you are enough, you are enough

Self-Praise is your self-love

Self-love is the best gift after all

You are you, nobody is like you

You are amazing, you are miraculous

You are love, you are everyone's beloved

So sing, dance and shine

Love yourself, consider your heart as your actual shrine

What Music Means To Me!

As I close my eyes and tune in

A force, almost like a rage starts to kick in

My heartbeat raises, igniting the fire within

My body moving, right from the head to the bottom of my feet

As my vocals starts to participate, a strong vibration takes me to a magical world

A world of freedom, creativity, fun, no concerns

This collaboration fans my flame

All I feel is music and me, dancing in rhythm, holding hands, feeling loved, feeling one, feeling free

I breathe music, I adore music

Music is a gateway, a portal for a universal connect

It is a common language, a beautiful communicator

It all started with music, it will end with music

My Life's Purpose

A guiding light that shines bright upon me

A cleansing energy that surrounds me

Filling me with love and warmth

This light is my sole guide to my life's purpose

To create incessant hope

To spread love limitlessly

To serve mother earth, to serve every life form

To always believe

To always stand for justice

Be an effective communicator

To exhibit acceptance

To advocate for kindness and compassion

To see what others see, to feel what others feel, to support those who need help

To send healing to those who are unwell

To see everyone on the same level, as equals

To devote part of my life to the public service

To guide, to connect

To share my work with the world

To raise my voice for the sufferers and those in pain

To be grateful to lord divine, to the universe and to my parents

To find a way to connect to the source

To entertain people

To honour my needs and others

To convoy enthusiasm

To educate regarding transformation

To always stay true to my words, use them wisely for the betterment of others

To encourage, to motivate

To always respect others and oneself

Inner Child

As I tap into the realm of my inner child

I see a beautiful innocent kid reaching out to me

A younger me!

We hold hands

Share a safe space of conversation

I listen, she talks

She listens as I talk

Her concerned look disappears

A happy excited face appears

Thanking me, embracing me

I cry and weep

Releasing all the burden

Healing myself and feeling loved again

Feeling strong again

Feeling happy again

Rewrite Your Story

Fire up your intention

Make a conscious decision

Look up, straight into the eye of crisis

Take a lead and move forward with utmost confidence

All you need is "you"

Unite with yourself, claim the power

Rewrite your own story

Breathe

There's more to life, more to the world

Take a pause, stop

Look in, focus

Inhale the refreshing air

Breathe in peace that's already within you

Exhale out the toxicity

Feel alive, Look alive

Spread your radiance and smile

Trade your cynical thoughts with the positive ones

A dose of confidence

A dose of hope

A dose of relaxation

A dose of calmness

A dose of love that's within you

A Therapy

A therapy of positive words

A therapy of positive thinking

A therapy of self-worthiness

A therapy of self-value

A blend of love and care

A list of all the self-praise

A variety of favourite food

Surrounded with favourite people

Traveling to bucket-listed places

Viewing a beautiful landscape

Feeling the air touching your cheeks, your hair
floating

A therapy of walking on the beach, waves touching
your feet

A therapy of experiencing a dog's love

A therapy of seeing a happy and smiling face of a kid

A therapy of pursuing your hobbies

A therapy of doing what you love

A therapy of gifting yourself with a "Me Time"

What I Stand For

I stand for myself

I stand for others

I stand for all those life forms who can't communicate like us

I stand for mother earth

I stand for people who have lost faith in themselves

I stand for love

I stand with people who believe in justice

I stand for change, transformation

I stand for what is right

I stand with people who need help and support

I stand for kindness

I stand for communication

I stand for being aware in awareness

The Value Of Little Things

The little things, glittering

A familiar voice that's calling in

That peaceful sleep on the mother's lap

The lecture of developing a constructive mindset by our beloved dad

That little fights with our siblings over who got the bigger piece?

The sound of first morning alarm that always goes on snooze

Sharing the lively moments with our best friends

Falling in love, heartbreak

Lots of pain and then regaining the power of ourselves

One moment we fall, another moment we rise

Every little thing has its value and meaning

Every little thing is beautiful and truthful

Rejection Is Redirection

We are imperfectionists and born to thrive

To learn, to grow, to expand

We can learn from mistakes

We can experiment and explore

So what if we fail?

So what if we are rejected?

We can still rise with more faith and determination

Rejection is a lesson

Rejection is Redirection

So lift up your spirits and regain yourself

Start, push and keep going!

A Questioning Spirit

We each have our own questions

In search of life's meaning

In the lookout for our purposes

To get to the root of subject matter

Why? When? How?

Makes us the most intelligent species

And an awakened one!

Follow Your Heart

Listen to what your heart has to say

Connect deep within

See what you love

Where your heart belongs

Follow your heart and re-start

Lead yourself to success

Lead yourself to real happiness

Your heart is your sole guide, a guardian angel

So fear no more, choose your actual path

And live your dream life!

The Sweet Emotion

Tapping into my well of childhood memories

Wrapping me with the sweet emotion of nostalgia

A world free of boundaries, stress and worries

A world of happiness, ice-cream, chocolates,
laughter and fun

Playing around a big healthy mango tree

Talking to imaginary friends

Dancing on any beat

Singing on our loudest voice

Composing music with forks and spoons

Collecting stamps, stones and coins

Creating our own wonderland in mind

Watching stars and moon

Peaceful sleep

The sweet emotion is all it is

The Voice

A million stories that our voice narrates

An expression of truth

An expression of love

List of emotions and feelings turning into words and sound

Using this voice to help, using this voice to protest

Make your voice hear loud and clear

So tone up and communicate the right messages

Your voice is power, your voice is strong!

The Sight

Open up your eyes

Observe the beautiful sky

The white clouds that look like cotton candy

The refreshing green colour of trees that soothes our eyes

The sight of the relaxing blue ocean

The birds flying from right to left and then in circle

A Black Labrador puppy playing with his toy

People busy making way to their destination

Kids playing happily in the garden

Everywhere I see is celebration

A sight of kindness

A sight of love

A sight of trust

A sight of argument

A sight of agreement

A sight of realization

A sight is beauty, a sight is peace

I am glad and blessed to have this precious vision

The Touch

Every touch takes me back to my memories

A flood of emotions

A flashback of yesterday

As I touch the window pane of my old house

I see it's colour gone dull, small scratches on the
sides

A childhood memory came rushing down

More than a memory, a realization to one of my life
purposes

A clarity to serve animal kingdom

My love for animals, my love for dogs

To feed them, to love them, to serve them

To hear their sweet little barks

To watch their heart melting puppy faces

Their eyes sparkling reminding me that its time!

Time for food, time for play, time for love

Every touch, every memory brings warmth

This touch deepens the gravity of our nostalgic feelings and emotions

A sense of love and relief surrounds us

I Hear

I hear that little voice talking to me

I call it as the voice of heart

Sometimes the voice of mind

It's like my own compass

It makes me sing and dance

Pushes me to care for my well-being

Sometimes stops me, sometimes directs me

Sometimes calms me

That little angelic voice I hear

The Feel

The feel of success

The feel of the knowing

The feel of words

The feel of heartbeat

The feel of touch

The feel of feelings

The feel of memories

The gravity of "feel" is beautiful

Like a roller coaster ride, exciting and empowering

A vibe, An aura, An experience of something unusual

The Fragrance Story

The fragrance of lavender scent

Takes my soul to its Mayfield

Visualizing its miraculous mesmerizing beauty

Its colour purple soothing my eyes, healing my
crown chakra

A feel of aromatic therapy

Inhaling the lavenderish air

A release of burden, a relief

A feel of calmness starts to kick in

The feather touch softness of the lavender plant

Turning on our playful mood

These peaceful moments, happy moments

Spreading love, radiating positivity and good vibes

Connecting fragrances to our old tales

Feeling fresh and refreshed

Connected and Nostalgic

Intoxicated with love!

These Waves

My heartbeats are blending with the sound of high
and low tides of the waves

I feel one with the sea

I feel loved

The soothing sound of the waves tickle my ears

The emitted energy from the sea enters my body
bringing me relief, bringing me freedom

A freedom of ideas, thoughts and actions

Colouring and activating my third eye chakra with
its blue

The love of white detaching me from all the burden
of negativity

Observing the waves coming towards me and then
returning

Touching my soul, my heart

Locking and un-locking me from its grasp

Taking me to the awe-inspiring experience of
watching these waves, the beautiful Arabian sea!

Let It Go

Whatever happened in the past, just let it go

Don't carry that burden in your present and future

Move on, go on

Forgive and forget, release

Believe in the power of "let it go"

Just flow, just flow!

Freedom

Freedom is happiness to create

Freedom is to express

Freedom is power to explore

Freedom is to design

Freedom is to act

Freedom is to love and fall in love

Freedom is to observe

Freedom is to care and share

Freedom is to spread kindness

Freedom is to live consciously and being aware

Joy

Joy is to enjoy a cup of my morning tea

Joy is to enjoy early sunlight

Joy is watching my mother's smile

Joy is to photograph

Joy is to write poetry

Joy is to sing and dance

Joy is to play the guitar

Joy is to smile and be happy for no reason

Speak Your Truth

What is your truth?

What is your reality?

Speak up, do not hesitate

Truth is the real treasure that makes life worth-living

Feel free by presenting your truth

Remedy

As I try to desperately find a place in this world

A place where I can be acknowledged

A place where I am valued

A place where people admire my true intentions

A place where I am not dishonoured

This desperation is making me feel like a fool

Like I am drowning

Numb and serious

Sleep deprived

In this series, music is my remedy

Takes me to my world of paradise

Tapping into my feelings and emotions that I didn't
know I have any more

Feeling loved again!

Infecting me with self-worth and patience

You are my remedy

Mom

You're my lifeline, my whole universe

You add meaning to my life

When you believe, I believe

When you smile, I smile

You support me when I don't deserve

You push me when I needed the most

Our communication is stronger like no other human

We are a team, a powerful force

You inspire me, you are a true angel

Thank you mom, I bow to you!

My Home

Home is in me

A space of comfort

A place of energy

Where happiness lies

Where peace can be find

Where there are no boundaries

No formalities

All there is love

Empathy

The moment we feel what others feel

The moment we understand what others are going through

The hardships, the heartbreaks

The happiness, the love

The testing situations

We share energies, we exchange words

We show our support

We empathize

Compassion

Compassion is care

Care for others

Our heart goes out for them

As if they are our own

We lend out our hands in support

We speak encouraging words

We hold hands, walk together

We spread oneness!

We spread love and kindness!

Courage

Courage is strength

To fight

To take a next step towards success

To follow your dreams

To stand against the odd

To believe in oneself

To stand strong for what you believe

To do what is right

To be an achiever

To be unstoppable

Accept Yourself

See who you are

Observe everything about you

Inspect, retrospect, introspect

Shed all the love on yourself

Accepting yourself is coming home

It is self-care

A devotion, a prayer

A foundation, your ideologies

Accept, believe and be confident

The Change

The change is unnerving but necessary

Challenging but interesting

It is a new era, a new course

Change is like a flowy water that keeps moving

It hurts to leave behind your old life, your old home, your old self

But keep moving is the moto

New chances, new scope, new ideas

New life, different people, different places

Different move, different thinking

The change then becomes your new home

Teaching you to never stop!

Success

The colours of success

A rainbow that shines on

A lot of hard work

A lot of thinking

An essence of creativity

Determination, Discipline, Dedication

A spirit of not giving up

A simple solution to each problem

Being fearless is all it takes

Observe

Observe a scene

A scene of everyday

Sitting in a cafe, looking out from a glass window

Watching people moving left to right and right to left and some crossing the road

Carrying briefcases, bags, coffee mugs in their hands

Observe a dog walking across the streets searching for some food in the wastebin

Observe the hustle in the lane, nobody stopping for no one

Observe huge buildings made of beautiful temperate glass

Look around you, the chairs and the tables made of Indian rosewood, a vintage theme

People talking, discussing, listening, holding hands, smiling, arguing, eating, drinking, coming and leaving

Their hand gestures, expressive eyes, restlessness, excitement, their calm, pore over

Now observe yourself, things surrounding you, your Montblanc notebook and pen, your phone, a cup of black coffee and chocolate muffin

Your thoughts, your self-talks, a trance state, a state of lucidity

We have so much to observe, so much to learn and so much to accept!

Sibling's Love

Growing up under your umbrella

Agreeing and disagreeing on small things

Fighting over silly things

Laughing together for no reason

A relationship of love and rivalry

I miss our pillow fights, the teasing, the complaining, the temporary cease fire

Everything you did, I did

Whether it's dancing or singing

Sharing secrets till late night

Riding together on that bright green bike

Apologizing when we were wrong

Advising and Suggesting

Supporting and Loving

All the time chit-chatting

Having a sister is a blessing

Because she will never leave your side!

Follow The Light

In the process of searching my own self

A process that leads to something unknown

Little unnerving, bit exciting

Somewhat stressful, yet relieving

When lost, be found

When trapped, unclasp yourself from the mind games

Just follow the sun

Just follow the light

Paradise

In the midst of the chaos

In the stressful difficult times

I close my eyes and travel to my own paradise

My personal heaven with soothing elements

Where I can communicate with the wild

A tiger showing me around

Birds singing me a song

Trees blessing me with love and light

A home within the mountains

The air, the breeze, the atmosphere of feeling free

Roaming around, touching the clouds

A mesmerizing view of nature

Praising mother earth

Filled up with spiritualism and divinity

Gratefulness and Love

No worries, no concerns

All I am is calm and happy

Photograph

A photograph that makes you smile

A photograph that makes you cry

A photograph that takes you back to those memories

Freezing that moment

Documenting your happiness

Narrating a story

Reviving feelings and emotions, old relations

An answer to your question

A freaking time machine

An ultimate healer

Night Sky

As I soak myself into the sight of constellations

Locks me in a state of trance

Bathing in the bright moonlight

Feeling the rise and fall of waves in my heart

Enjoying every moment of stargazing

Imagining the beauty of nebulae

Born and made of stardust

The universal elements rushing through my veins

A feel of connect

A feel of love

A feel of vastness

A realization of universe living within us

A feeling of oneness with the night sky and the universe

Balance

A spinning wheel coloured in red

A state of equilibrium

A foundation of us and our energies

A sense of security

A sense of stability

A connection to mother earth

A connection to our belonging and survival

Hero

A hero that resides in all of us

Who's a saviour, a protector, a lover

Who's the main lead yet play different parts

That hero who act, voice out when things are not right, fight, care, share

We don't need superheroes

All we need is a superhuman

That we all are!

So activate your inner hero

Bring the humility, the empathy, the kindness into this world

You are brave, you are strong

You have all the elements to thrive

Protect mother earth, protect your people

Connect and Communicate

Motivate and Inspire

And Pass it on!

Love

Open up your heart

Define your version of love

Love is freedom

Love is beautiful

Uplift your spirits

See new possibilities

Feel the love

Feel the life

Blend with love

And set yourself free

That's the power of love

A magical four letter word

A common language

A symbol of peace

A magnificent energy!

Mother Earth

A source of life

A home to millions of creatures

A giver, A nurturer

A symbol of motherhood, a creator

Her beautiful green hair protects us during extensive heat

Also the food for other species

The sea, the ocean is her lovely smile

She shares her water to farm and eradicate thirst

Her fertile land helps us grow our food

She shows her happiness through the changing seasons

And her rage through storms and hurricane

Forest fires and earthquake

The nature always communicates through her landscape and wildlife

Even in these changing times, she is speaking

Showing signs to stop the overuse and exploitation

To give back, return

To restore our humanity, reclaim the long
lost humility

To take care of other creatures, the animal kingdom

To look after this precious amazing planet, our only
home

Asking us to treat her with dignity and love

And to save our injured planet!

Expansion

Expansion is growth

A new learning, new lessons, knowledge and wisdom

Expansion is broadening your horizon

Expansion is a greater reach

A source to new ideas, lucidity, new concepts

To new dimension, to new hacks

An expansion within ourselves

An expansion through our third eye chakra

A tinch of indigo blue

A medium of light!

Dance

A rhythmic movement

A flow of emotions

An art of expression

A release of energy

A head-heart collaboration

Communicating a message

A space where you are safe

Pouring with feelings of loss, love and happiness

Regaining power and strength

A reunion with the lost freedom

Flying and floating

Letting all go

Release and Surrender

The Instinct

A divine guidance

Our superpower

The most important voice

That instinctive feeling

Our internal soothsayer

A knower, A second sight

Trust your intuition

Listen to it

It's your ultimate director!

These Words

These words die as soon as we speak

An invisible sword and shield

These words hurt and heal

No sound we hear as they collide

All we hear is the sound of our voice

These words starts a war

These words stops a fight

These words makes us smile

These words make us cry

Sometimes uplifts us

Sometimes disappoints

A source of chaos, a source of peace

It's strength is marvellous that is all we can feel

Sometimes it rip us apart, sometimes bring us close

Words touch our heart and soul

Forces us to imagine back and forth

It's power is impeccable that's beyond our

visualization

All we know is these words are our true source of

language and communication

A wonderful source of expression!

Everest

A jewel of the great himalayas

Sagarmatha, a peak of heaven

An impeccable beauty

Narrating a thousand stories

A witness to various victorious and tragic moments

A home to imaginary abominables

A goal and love of millions of mountaineers

A pride of Everest submitters

An eye-lock scenic landscape

A thin breeze that can take you in its grasp

A feeling of upliftment

Full of drama, a deep sense of reverence!

Support

Like floating on the water

Like the support of the ground

A synonym to encouragement

A dose of enthusiasm

The Earthly support

The Universal support

A support of your loved ones

A support of oneself

This support is a portal to success

A portal to that unknown power within oneself

The End

Look around, look in, fall in love, explore, experience, be open, be receiving, be kind to self, to others, to mother nature, be compassionate, have faith in yourself, in lord divine, in the universe and always be hopeful!

www.ingramcontent.com/pod-product-compliance
Lightning Source LLC
LaVergne TN
LVHW050418160726
843469LV00041B/1128